# Lebanese

March 2010

W9-BFJ-704

## TARLA DALAL

India's # 1 Cookery Author

S&C
SANJAY & CO.
MUMBAI

First Printing : 2007

ISBN : 978-8-189491-52-9

**Copyright © Sanjay & Co.**

"Tarla Dalal" is also a registered trademark owned by Sanjay & Co.

All rights reserved with the publishers.

No part of this book may be reproduced, stored in a retrieval system or transmitted by any means, electronic, mechanical, photocopying, recording or otherwise, without the written permission of the publishers.

**Price: Rs. 89/-**

Published & Distributed by : **Sanjay & Company**

353/ A-1, Shah & Nahar Industrial Estate, Dhanraj Mill Compound, Lower Parel (W), Mumbai - 400 013. INDIA.
Tel. : (91-22) 2496 8068 • Fax : (91-22) 2496 5876 • E-mail : sanjay@tarladalal.com

---

**UK and USA customers can call us on :**

UK : 02080029533　　●　　USA : 213-634-1406

For books, Membership on **tarladalal.com**, Subscription for **Cooking & More** and Recipe queries
**Timing :** 9.30 a.m. to 7.00 p.m. (IST), from Monday to Saturday
*Local call charges applicable*

---

| Recipe Research & Production Design | Nutritionists | Photography | Designed by | Copy Editing |
|---|---|---|---|---|
| Arati Fedane | Nisha Katira | Jignesh Jhaveri | Satyamangal Rege | Janani Gopalakrishnan |
| Kunal Patil | Sapna Kamdar | | | |
| Pragnesh Joshi | | | | |
| | **Food Styling** | **Typesetting** | **Printed by :** | |
| | Shubhangi Dhaimade | Adityas Enterprises | Minal Sales Agencies, Mumbai | |

**DISCLAIMER**
While every precaution has been taken in the preparation of this book, the publishers and the author assume no responsibility for errors or omissions. Neither is any liability assumed for damages resulting from the use of information contained herein. And of course, no book is a substitute for a qualified medical advice. So it is wiser to modify your dietary patterns under the supervision of a doctor or a nutritionist.

**BULK PURCHASES**
Tarla Dalal Cookbooks are ideal gifts. If you are interested in buying more than 500 assorted copies of Tarla Dalal Cookbooks at special prices, please contact us at 91-22-2496 8068 or email : sanjay@tarladalal.com

FRESH FRUIT GATEAU

PHOTOGRAPH BY JIGNESH JHAVERI

# TARLA DALAL

INDIA'S # 1 COOKERY AUTHOR

OVER 3,50,000 REGISTERED MEMBERS

BECOME A GOLD

OR SILVER MEMBER

ON TARLADALAL.COM

AND FIND ALL YOUR

FAVOURITE RECIPES.

For further information mail us at
tarla@tarladalal.com
or call on our helpline no. 022-2496 8068
on all weekdays between
9.30 am and 4.30 pm.

# INTRODUCTION

Hello Friends,

After a long time I bring to you a book completely dedicated to a particular foreign cuisine. This time it's **Lebanese,** one of the cuisines from Middle East regions. Personally witnessing the rise of Falafel and Hummus in India I thought its time for some additions to this list and let you know more about Lebanese.

To start with, the invigorating food of Lebanon is a great combination of health and pleasure. Lebanese is a fusion cuisine that combines the best aspects of European and Arabic cooking styles to produce a winning combination. I know most of us associate Middle Eastern cuisines with meat and expensive ingredients. But you will be surprised to know that Lebanese is one of the cuisines from this region that boats of most popular vegetarian dishes and at the same time is fresh and light.

The 47 mouth-watering recipes in this book have been divided as per courses like Appetizers (Mezze), Soups & Salads, Main courses, Rice dishes, Desserts and Beverages. A few recipes are modified as per the Indian palate and some are my own creations using Lebanese ingredients.

The first few pages of the book will give you an insight about the cuisine, its cooking styles, the ingredients used and every such detail. Follow them religiously and I am sure you will master Lebanese recipes in no time.

All the best.

# CONTENTS

## MEZZE (APPETIZERS)

## SOUPS & SALADS

## *Introduction*

*L*ebanon - a country whose capital was once referred to as the Paris of Middle East was indeed an ideal tourist destination because of its golden beaches, snow clad mountains, homely culture and healthy cuisine. Today, however, think of Lebanon and all that comes to your mind is war & destruction. But inspite of all the unfortunate incidents nothing has stopped the fresh and light cuisine of Lebanon to spread successfully across the globe.

Lebanese is a fusion cuisine that combines the best aspects of European and Arabic cooking styles to produce a winning combination. It uses all exotic ingredients yet is light on the stomach. It satiates you completely without the guilt of eating fat laden food. A large and varied assortment of vegetables and fresh fruits accompany the above, and meat plays a relatively small part. Unlike other Middle Eastern cuisines, Lebanese cuisine takes pride in producing some of the most famous **vegetarian** dishes like Hummus, Tabbouleh and Falafel. It emphasizes more on cereals, herbs, grains and milk products.

The invigorating food of Lebanon is a great combination of health and pleasure.

# *Typical Lebanese Meal*

A traditional beginning to a Lebanese meal would be with **arak**, an aniseed flavoured liqueur. The drinks are a gentle lead up to the mezze (appetizers) - a spread of many small hot and cold dishes. The **Mezze** may be as simple as pickled vegetables, hummus and bread, or it may become an entire meal consisting of grilled marinated seafood, skewered meats, a variety of cooked and raw salads, and an arrangement of desserts.

No Lebanese meal would be complete without serving breads. Lebanese have mastered the art of baking unleavened breads, which are now forming a part of many Western cusines too. Pita, the famous sandwich bread, is also eaten during meals where it replaces the fork and spoon. Lavash, a crisp bread is usually served with dips like Baba ganoush or Labneh.

**Baklava**, a renowned sweet from Lebanon is often served as dessert along with coffee. The Lebanese baklava consists of layers of filo pastry drenched in sugar syrup and generously served with nuts. Sweet marts in Middle East sell baklava with over 20 varieties, which are also exported on a large scale to the European markets.

## *The Lebanese Pantry*

Stack your kitchen with the ingredients mentioned in the Lebanese pantry list and prepare any Lebanese creation in no time.

* **Spices & herbs :** Mint and parsley are most extensively used herbs. Cumin and cardamom spices come next. A special spice blend called "Baharat" is freshly prepared and always kept handy. You can follow the recipe on page 101.

* **Tahini paste :** Made from toasted sesame seeds, it is used in many dishes and sauces such as Hummus, page 20 and Falafel, page 13. At times small amounts of sugar or molasses are added to it to make a sweet snack with flat pita bread. The Indian markets have recently been stocked with readymade Tahini paste bottles. If you are one of those tied on time when it comes to food, then this could be a nice short cut for you, else try the recipe on page 17.

* **Pita bread :** A staple bread for the Lebanese, Pita bread makes an appearance at almost every meal. Try our easy version on page 99.

* **Yoghurt** : One of the cornerstones of Lebanese cooking. Even though decent plain yogurt can be bought, you should try to make your own at least once. It is used as-is, in cooking, as a sauce base or to make a delicious yogurt cheese called Labneh, page 27.

* **Rose water** : This is one of the ingredients for most Lebanese desserts. Here, rose water is extracted from a very fragrant pink rose called **'Wardi el Jooriya'**. Apart from its royal flavour rose water also helps to give a cooling effect.

## Mezze ( Appetizers )

# Falafel

**Picture on cover.**

*Falafel is an assembled mezze of chick pea patties sandwiched between pita bread. This popular sandwich has found place in most restaurant menus across the globe. The sandwich can be moistened with some of our desi green chutney or either by authentic Lebanese garlic sauce.*

Preparation Time: 10 minutes.   Cooking Time: 15 minutes.   Serves 4.
Soaking Time: Overnight.

**For the *patties***
½ cup *kabuli chana* (chick peas)
¼ cup chopped onions
1 tbsp chopped garlic
2 tbsp finely chopped parsley (both leaf and stem)
½ tsp cumin seeds (*jeera*) powder
½ tsp baharat, page 101
1 tbsp finely chopped mint leaves (*phudina*)
1 tbsp finely chopped coriander (*dhania*)
Salt to taste
Oil for deep-frying

**For the dressing**
⅓ cup fresh curds (dahi), whisked
2 cloves garlic, chopped
¼ cup chopped spring onions
(including greens)
a pinch of sugar
Salt to taste

**Other ingredients**

6 pita breads, page 99
½ cup thinly sliced tomatoes
1 cup shredded lettuce

**For the patties**
1. Soak the *kabuli chana* in water overnight. Clean, wash and drain.
2. Blend in a mixer to a coarse paste.
3. Add all the remaining ingredients and mix well.
4. Divide the mixture into 30 equal portions and shape each portion into small balls.
5. Heat the oil in a *kadhai* and deep-fry the balls till they turn golden brown. Drain on absorbent paper.

**For the dressing**
Blend all the ingredients in a mixer to a smooth sauce. Keep aside.

**How to proceed**
1. Cut each pita bread into two and warm the halves on a hot griddle (tava).
2. Fill each pita bread half with some tomato slices and shredded lettuce, a few patties and a spoonful of the dressing on top.
3. Repeat for the remaining pita bread halves and other ingredients to make 11 more falafels. Serve immediately.

# *Lavash*

**Picture on page 1.**

*Lavash is a crisp bread resembling the Indian khakra. It is made with maida and topped with roasted sesame seeds and poppy seeds.*

Preparation Time: 10 minutes.   Cooking Time: 45 minutes.   Makes approx. 25 chips.
Baking Temperature: 180°C (360°F).   Baking Time: 15 minutes.

¾ cup plain flour (*maida*)
½ tsp dry yeast
A pinch sugar
4 tbsp roasted sesame seeds (*til*)
3 tbsp poppy seeds (*khus-khus*)
2½ tbsp olive oil or oil
Salt to taste

1. Combine the yeast and sugar with ½ cup of warm water in a bowl. Cover and keep aside till it becomes frothy. (approx. 10 minutes.)

2. Sift the flour. Make a well in the centre and add the yeast and sugar mixture and enough water to make a soft dough. This will take about 7 minutes.
3. Keep the dough for 30 minutes under a wet cloth till it doubles in volume.
4. Divide the dough into 5 equal portions and roll each portion into a circle of 150 mm. (6") diameter. Cut each circle into 5 equal triangles. Repeat with the remaining portions to make 20 more triangles.
5. Brush each triangle with a little oil and sprinkle some sesame seeds and poppy seeds on top.
6. Arrange these triangles on a greased baking tray and bake in a pre-heated oven at 180°C (360°F) for 10 minutes or till the chips turn golden brown.

**HANDY TIP:** If you do not want to use the oven, just dry roast the dough triangles on a *tava* on both sides using a kitchen towel to flatten it as done for making *khakhras*.

# Tahini Dip

*An inseparable part of Lebanese cuisine, Tahini basically means a paste of roasted sesame (til) seeds. The paste is widely used to make salad dressings, dips and sauces. In the given recipe it is combined with curds which results in a unique bitter-sour product. Besides pita bread, as suggested, the dip goes well with pita bread, page 99 or lavash, page 15.*

Preparation Time: 20 minutes.   Cooking Time: 15 minutes.   Makes 1 cup.
Baking Temperature: 180°C (360°F).   Baking Time: 15 minutes.

1½ cups fresh curds (*dahi*)
Salt to taste

**For the Tahini paste**
2 tbsp sesame seeds (*til*)
2 tbsp lemon juice
2 tbsp olive oil
½ tsp finely chopped garlic
Salt to taste

**For serving**
Pita bread, page 99 or Lavash, page 15

**For the Tahini paste**
1. Roast the sesame seeds on a *tava* (griddle) for a few seconds.
2. Cool, add all the remaining ingredients and blend in a mixer to a smooth paste.

**How to proceed**
1. Hang the curds in a muslin cloth for 15 minutes.
2. Whisk till smooth and add the Tahini paste and salt if required.
3. Whisk again and refrigerate till ready to use.
   Serve immediately with pita bread or lavash.

ARABIC SALAD : Recipe on page 49 ● TABBOULEH : Recipe on page 47. →

# Hummus

**Picture on page 1.**

*Here is one more exotic dip from Lebanon. Like most dips this is curd cased too with an unusual paste of boiled chick peas. The dip is quite bland but is definitely a good choice for weight watchers. Again pair it with pita or some garden fresh vegetable sticks.*

Preparation Time: 20 minutes.   Cooking Time: 15 minutes.   Makes 1½ cups.
Soaking Time: Overnight.

1 cup *kabuli chana* (chick peas)
Salt to taste
1 tbsp chopped garlic
2 tbsp lemon juice
2 tsp tahini paste, page 17
¼ cup fresh curds (*dahi*)
2 tbsp olive oil
½ tbsp chopped parsley, ¼ tsp chilli powder and 2 tsp olive oil for the garnish

**For serving**
Pita bread, page 99
Vegetable sticks (Carrots, french beans, celery, zucchini etc.)

1. Soak the *kabuli chana* in water overnight. Clean, wash and drain.
2. Add 1 cup of water and salt and pressure cook till the *kabuli chana* is overcooked.
3. Drain and reserve the liquid.
4. Blend the *chana* along with the garlic, lemon juice, tahini paste, curds, salt and olive oil in a mixer to a smooth paste. If the mixture is too thick add 2 to 3 tbsp of the reserved liquid.
5. Place this mixture in a serving plate, garnish with parsley, chilli powder and olive oil and refrigerate till ready to use.
   Serve chilled with pita bread.

**HANDY TIP:** You can use the readymade tahini paste available in the market which will in fact lend a better falvour.

# Baba Ganoush

**Picture on page 1.**

*Lebanon has a few favourites amongst the vegetable group and brinjal is one of them. It is so relished that apart from being grilled and served as main course, the vegetable is also ground to a paste and converted to a delicious dip. This dip can easily be termed as an uncooked version of our baingan bharta. Off course, the brinjal is cooked but the remaining ingredients are added raw maintaining the tradition of healthy eating. Remove the tahini paste and you will get another dip called* **"Moutabel"**.

Preparation Time: 20 minutes.   Cooking Time: 15 minutes.   Makes 1½ cups.
Baking Temperature: 170°C (340°F).   Baking Time: 25 minutes.

4 to 6 medium dark skinned brinjals (*baingan* / eggplant)
1 tsp olive oil
5 tsp tahini paste, page 17
1 tsp copped garlic
½ tsp cumin seeds (*jeera*) powder
1 tbsp lemon juice
Salt to taste
1 tsp chopped coriander (*dhania*) for the garnish
Oil for greasing

22

**For serving**
Thinly sliced bread, toasted

1. Grease the brinjals with a little oil, place on a baking tray and bake in pre-heated oven at 170°C (340°F) till the skin is chared and the brinjal is tender (approx. 20 minutes).
2. Cool, peel and discard the skin and mash the brinjals to a pulp.
3. Add all the remaining ingredients and mix well.
   Garnish with coriander and serve with toasted bread slices.

# Red Capsicum and Walnut Dip

**Picture on page 1.**

*Quite a rare combination of vegetables with nuts. The appetizing red colour will develop a flavour in your mind even before you taste it. Remember to wash off the burnt skin of the capsicum before blending it or else it will lend a bitter flavour to the dish.*

Preparation Time: 15 minutes.   Cooking Time: 7-8 minutes.   Makes ¾ cup.

1 red capsicum
½ tsp finely chopped green chillies
2 tbsp toasted bread crumbs
½ cup roughly chopped walnuts (*akhrot*)
1 tsp lemon juice
1 tbsp pomegranate (*anar*) juice
¼ tsp cumin seeds (*jeera*) powder
¼ tsp sugar
Salt to taste
2 tsp olive oil

**For serving**
Sesame Lavash, page 15

1. Pierce a fork through the red capsicum and roast on an open flame for about 7 to 8 minutes or till the skin is charred. Keep aside to cool.
2. Peel off the blackened skin, cut in to 4 pieces and remove the seeds.
3. Wash well, add all the remaining ingredients and blend in a mixer to a smooth paste.
   Serve with sesame lavash.

# Labanese Mayonnaise

*It's actually known as **"Lebanese Garlic Sauce"** but we have taken the liberty to change the name so it is easily understood. Garlic is one spice the Lebanese love to eat. The sauce is made mayonnaise style using the technique of oil emulsion in potatoes and not eggs. The garlic sauce can be used as an accompaniment to grilled vegetables or as a spread on pita.*

Preparation Time: 5 minutes.   Cooking Time: 10 minutes.   Makes 1 cup.

¼ cup finely chopped garlic
3 tbsp lemon juice
2 tbsp boiled, peeled and mashed potatoes
Salt to taste
½ tsp white pepper powder
1 cup oil

1. Combine the garlic, lemon juice, potatoes, salt and pepper powder together blend in a mixer to a smooth paste.
2. Remove into a bowl, add the oil in a very slow stream while whisking continuously using a whisk till it gets the consistency of mayonnaise.
3. Refrigerate in a glass container and use as required.

# Labneh Stuffed Olives

Labneh is a tangy dip which is usually served as is with pita bread for breakfast or snacks. In the given recipe, it is stuffed in olives to create a quick and lovely looking mezze dish. Labneh can be spiced with baharat powder to make the dish a bit spicy.

If you are not too diet conscious add a bit of cream to the Labneh for a better texture. For good presentation you can slice the stuffed olives and serve on a bed of shredded purple cabbage.

Preparation Time: 10 minutes.   Cooking Time: 5 minutes.   Makes 25 stuffed olives.

25 large deseeded green olives
1 tsp extra virgin olive oil

**To be mixed together for the labneh**
4 tbsp thick hung curds (*chakka*)
1 tsp fresh cream
1 clove garlic, grated
Salt to taste

1. Fill the olives with the prepared labneh.
2. Drizzle a little olive oil on them and serve at room temperature.

# *Khyaar Bi Leban* (Cucumber and Yogurt Dip)

*All this dip sums up to is cool and refreshing... perfect for summer cocktail parties.*

Preparation Time: 5 minutes.   Cooking Time: Nil.   Serves 4.

2 cups fresh hung curds (*chakka*)
2 tbsp finely chopped garlic
Salt to taste
1 tsp freshly ground pepper
2 tsp finely chopped mint leaves (*phudina*)
½ cup finely chopped cucumber

**For serving**
Pita bread, page 99

1. Whisk the curds till smooth.
2. Add the garlic, salt, pepper and mint leaves and whisk again.
3. Add the cucumber and mix well.
4. Refrigerate till use.
   Serve chilled with pita bread.

# Muhhamarra

*This spicy, nutty walnut and red chilli paste that is a little like humus in texture. It makes an unusual dip.*

Preparation Time: 5 minutes.   Cooking Time: Nil.   Makes approx. 1½ cup.

¾ cup chopped walnuts
2 tsp chopped garlic
½ cup fresh breadcrumbs
2 whole dry Kashmiri red chillies
1 tbsp pomegranate molasses / anardana
¼ cup olive oil / oil
Salt to taste

1. Soak the dry red chillies in warm water for about 30 minutes. Drain and discard the water.
2. Combine all the ingredients including the red chillies and blend to a smooth paste.
3. Serve with pita bread, lavoush or strips of vegetables like cucumber, carrots, zucchini etc.

# Spinach Sambousik

*Tiny half moon shaped savouries stuffed with a spinach-pine nut mixture and deep fried. A must in the mezze platter.*

Preparation Time: 20 minutes.  Cooking Time: 15 minutes.  Makes 10 sambousiks.

**For the dough**
1 cup plain flour (*maida*)
Salt to taste
3 tbsp melted ghee (*samneh*)

**For the spinach and cheese filling**
2 tsp oil
½ cup chopped onions
2 cloves garlic, chopped
½ cup chopped tomatoes
Salt to taste
½ tsp baharat, page 101
1 cup blanched and chopped spinach (*palak*)
2 tbsp roasted and chopped pine nuts (chilgoza)
½ cup grated cheese

**Other ingredients**
Oil for deep frying

**For the dough**
1. Sieve the flour, mix with melted ghee and salt and add enough cold water to make a firm dough.
2. Knead for sometime till smooth.

3. Cover and keep aside.

**For spinach and cheese filling**
1. Heat the oil in a pan, add the onions and garlic and sauté for 2 minutes.
2. Add the tomatoes and salt and cook for a further 5 minutes.
3. Add all the remaining ingredients except the cheese and sauté for 2 more minutes or till the mixture dries.
4. Remove from the flame and add the grated cheese.
5. Mix well and divide into 10 equal portions. Keep aside.

**How to proceed**
1. Divide the dough into 10 equal portions.
2. Roll out each portion into a 75 mm. (3") diameter circle.
3. Place one portion of the filling in the centre of each circle.
4. Gently fold the circle into a semicircle and seal the edges.
5. To decorate the edges, twist the edges carefully with the thumb and forefinger like a *ghugra*. Alternatively cut with a decorative cutter.
6. Repeat steps 2-5 to make 9 more sambousiks.
7. Heat the oil in a *kadhai* and deep-fry the sambousiks in it on a medium flame till they are golden brown in colour.
8. Drain on absorbent paper and serve hot.

# Mezze Platter

*An assorted platter of snacks dips salads and breads. The main-stay of Lebanese cuisine.*

Preparation Time: 10 minutes.    Cooking Time: Nil.    Serves 4.

¼ cup Hummus, page 20
¼ cup Baba Ganoush, page 22
¼ cup Red Capsicum and Walnut Dip, page 24
1 cup Tabbouleh, page 47
1 cup Fattoush, page 45
4 pita breads, page 99, lightly toasted and cut into smaller pieces
4 lavash, page 15
A few thin slices of bread, toasted or plain
4 Falafel, page 13
4 Spinach Sambousiks, page 30
¼ cup pickled vegetables, page 51
A few lettuce leaves

Divide all the ingredients into 4 equal portions and arrange them on 4 large platters. Serve immediately.

# Soups & Salads

# Rice Soup

*A thick soup delicately flavoured with fresh mint leaves. The soup is also called "**yalya soup**".
The mint leaves can be dried before hand and stored in an air-tight container.*

Preparation Time: 5 minutes.   Cooking Time: 20 minutes.   Serves 4.

½ cup fresh mint leaves (*phudina*)
¼ cup rice
1 cup fresh curds (*dahi*)
2 tbsp cornflour dissolved in 2 tbsp of water
Salt to taste

1. Heat a non stick pan and dry roast the mint leaves until crisp. Keep aside
2. Boil 3 cups of water in a broad pan, add the rice and cook till it is done.
3. Add another 1½ cups of water, curds and cornflour mixture and cook for a few minutes.
4. Add the dried mint and salt and simmer for 2 minutes.
   Serve hot.

# Spinach and Lentil Soup

Picture on page 37.

*As we know Lebanese food is very much healthy and nutritious, this is one such light on the stomach soup from their cuisine. With no calories but only goodness of red lentils and spinach the soup is a dieter's delight.*

Preparation Time: 10 minutes.   Cooking Time: 1 hour 25 minutes.   Serves 4.
Soaking Time: 3 hours.

1 cup *masoor dal* (split red lentils)
2 tbsp oil
½ cup chopped onions
2 tsp chopped garlic
1 tsp cumin seeds (*jeera*) powder
Salt to taste
¼ tsp sugar
6 cups vegetable stock, page 102
1 cup shredded spinach (*palak*)
¼ cup chopped coriander (*dhania*)
1 tsp lemon rind

1 tsp lemon juice

1. Soak the *masoor dal* for about 3 hours. Wash, drain and keep aside.
2. Heat the oil in a broad pan, add the onions and garlic and sauté till the onions turn golden brown
3. Add the *masoor dal,* cumin seeds powder, salt, sugar and vegetable stock and cook it till the *dal* is tender.
4. Add the spinach, coriander, lemon rind and lemon juice and mix well.
5. Simmer for a few minutes and serve hot.

**SPINACH AND LENTIL SOUP : Recipe on page 35. →**

# *Tomato Vermicelli Soup*

*Who doesn't love tomatoes? Yes, this cuisine also has its own version of tomato soup which has an addition of thin noodles. Quick to prepare, the soup is seasoned with freshly ground pepper that makes it ideal for winters.*

Preparation Time: 10 minutes.   Cooking Time: 15 minutes.   Serves 4.

1 tbsp oil
2 tsp chopped garlic
2 tbsp chopped onions
¾ cup chopped tomatoes
1 tbsp tomato purée
Salt to taste
½ tsp freshly ground black pepper
3 cups vegetable stock, page 102
2 tbsp vermicelli, broken into pieces
1 tbsp fresh cream
2 tbsp chopped parsley for the garnish

1. Heat the oil in a broad pan, add the garlic and onions and sauté till the onions turn translucent.
2. Add the tomatoes and sauté for another 2 minutes.
3. Add the tomato purée, salt, pepper and vegetable stock and bring to boil.
4. Lower the flame and simmer for 15 minutes.
5. Remove from the flame, allow to cool and blend in a mixer till smooth.
6. Pour the mixture back into the pan, add the vermicelli and simmer till the vermicelli is cooked.
7. Add the cream and mix well.
   Serve hot garnished with parsley.

# Vegetable Soup

*Well now this is not the usual vegetable soup that you make often for your family. The way of preparation remains unchanged but ingredients used are quite different. Vegetables used are only zucchini and carrots while the baharat powder completely alters the taste of this soup.*

Preparation Time: 10 minutes.   Cooking Time: 25 minutes.   Serves 4.

2 tbsp oil
2 tsp chopped garlic
2 tbsp chopped onions
¼ tsp baharat, page 101
Salt to taste
½ tsp freshly ground black pepper
¼ cup chopped tomatoes
5 cups vegetable stock, page 102
¼ cup sliced zucchini
¼ cup peeled and sliced carrots
2 tsp chopped celery
3 tbsp chopped parsley

**For serving**
Pita bread, page 99

1. Heat the oil in a pan add the garlic and onions and sauté till the onions turn translucent.
2. Add the baharat, salt, black pepper and tomatoes and sauté for another 2 minutes.
3. Add the vegetable stock and bring to boil.
4. Lower the flame and add the zucchini, carrots and celery.
5. Cover the pan with a lid and allow to simmer for about 20 minutes or till the vegetables are cooked.
6. Add the parsley and mix well.
   Serve hot with pita bread.

# Chick Pea Soup

*Lebanese know how to use their favourite chick peas in all possible manner. Presenting here is a soup made from this lentil which is flavoured with the spicy baharat powder and enriched with fragrant cardamom.*

Preparation Time: 10 minutes.   Cooking Time: 25 minutes.   Serves 4.

¼ cup boiled *kabuli chana* (chick peas)
1 tbsp ghee (*samneh*)
2 crushed cardamoms (*elaichi*)
½ cup finely chopped onions
1 tbsp finely chopped garlic
½ cup potatoes cubes
½ cup chopped tomatoes
½ tsp baharat, page 101
Salt to taste
1 tbsp tomato purée
1 tsp lemon juice
½ cup chopped parsley
2 tbsp grated cheddar cheese for the garnish

1. Heat the ghee in a broad pan, add cardamoms and sauté for about 30 seconds.
2. Add the onions and garlic and sauté till the onions turn golden brown.
3. Add the potatoes, tomatoes, baharat, salt and 4 cups of water and cook it till the potatoes are tender.
4. Add the tomato purée, lemon juice, *kabuli chana* and parsley. Mix well and simmer for 2 to 3 minutes.
5. Serve hot garnished with cheddar cheese.

# Potato Salad

*Soft potato cubes tossed in a palatable dressing made out of pomegranate powder and lemon juice. Parsley is used in huge amounts as the Lebanese love this herb.*

Preparation Time: 10 minutes.   Cooking Time: No cooking.   Serves 4.

3 large potatoes, boiled
½ cup chopped onions
1 tbsp finely chopped garlic
1 tsp freshly ground black pepper
¼ cup finely chopped parsley
2 tbsp finely chopped mint leaves (*phudina*)

2 tbsp lemon juice
½ tsp pomegranate seeds (*anardana*) powder
2 tbsp olive oil
Salt to taste

1. Peel the potatoes and cut into small cubes.
2. Add all the remaining ingredients and toss well.
3. Refrigerate till use.
   Serve chilled.

# Fattoush

*A one of its kind salad by the Lebanese that uses pita bread along with unique vegetables like radish and spring onions to create a crunchy and crisp final product. Remember to toss the bread with the dressing only few minutes before you serve it or else the bread will soak the liquid and turn chewy.*

Preparation Time: 10 minutes.   Cooking Time: 1-2 minutes.   Serves 4.

1 pita bread, page 99
1 cup cucumber cubes
1 cup tomato cubes
½ cup red capsicum cubes
1 cup iceberg lettuce, torn into pieces
¼ cup finely chopped parsley
¼ cup chopped mint leaves (*phudina*)
½ cup thinly sliced radish
¼ cup thinly sliced spring onion whites
¼ cup finely chopped spring onion greens

**To be mixed into a dressing**
2 tbsp olive oil

2 tbsp lemon juice
Salt to taste
1 tsp freshly ground pepper
1 tbsp chopped garlic

1. Toast the pita bread on *tava* (griddle) till it turns golden brown and crisp.
2. Break into small pieces and keep aside.
3. Combine all the ingredients except the bread and toss well.
4. Refrigerate to chill.
5. Just before serving, combine the bread and dressing and toss well.
   Serve immediately.

# Tabbouleh

**Picture on page 19.**

*An inseparable part of mezze, this exclusive broken wheat salad is flavoured with sesame seeds.*
*A landmark dish for the Lebanese cuisine, which combines most of its favourites like parsley, mint,*
*olive oil and lemon juice. You can add a few citrus fruit pieces to create a fruity variation.*

Preparation Time: 15 minutes.   Cooking Time: 10 minutes.   Serves 4.

1 cup broken wheat (*dalia*)
¼ cup finely chopped mint leaves (*phudina*)
½ cup finely chopped parsley
2 tbsp toasted sesame seeds (*til*)
¼ cup finely chopped spring onion (greens and whites)
½ cup finely chopped tomatoes
2 tbsp lemon juice
2 tbsp olive oil
Salt to taste

1. Boil 1½ cups of water in a broad pan, add the broken wheat and cook for 10
   minutes or till it is tender.

2. Drain and pour cold water over it to cool the broken wheat. Drain again and keep aside.
3. Combine all the ingredients including the broken wheat in a bowl and mix well.
4. Refrigerate for at least 1 hour before serving so that all the flavours blend.
   Serve chilled.

# Arabic Salad

**Picture on page 19.**

*The salad is traditionally flavoured with sumac powder, which is a Middle Eastern spice made from the berries of the sumac bush. The powder has a tart flavour thus we have substituted it with pomegranate powder and lemon juice. It is worth hunting down if you possibly can. But the salad is equally delicious even if you can't find it.*

Preparation Time: 5 minutes.   Cooking Time: Nil.   Serves 4.

1 cup iceberg lettuce, torn into pieces
½ cup cherry tomatoes, halved
½ cup cucumber cubes
5 green olives
5 black olives
½ cup chopped mint leaves (*phudina*)

**To be mixed into a dressing**
2 tbsp lemon juice
½ tsp baharat, page 101
¼ tsp pomegranate (*anardana*) powder
Salt to taste

Combine all the ingredients, pour the dressing on top and serve immediately.

# Spinach and Nut Salad

*A salad that is nutty enough to leave you asking for more. The combination of walnuts with a tangy dressing and bland spinach leaves is quite a creation to try out.*

Preparation Time: 10 minutes.   Cooking Time: 10 minutes.   Serves 4.

1 cup tender spinach leaves (*palak*)
½ cup blanched French beans, cut into 1" pieces
½ cup chopped walnuts (*akhrot*)
¼ cup sliced onions

**To be mixed into a dressing**
2 tbsp chopped mint leaves. (*phudina*)
2 tsp lemon juice
¼ tsp pomegranate (*anardana*) powder
Salt to taste
2 tbsp olive oil

Combine all the ingredients in a bowl, pour the dressing and toss well.
Serve immediately.

# Pickled Vegetables

*A spicy and sour accompaniment to mezze dishes. The vegetables compliment many a bland dishes served as mezze.*

Preparation Time: 10 minutes.  Cooking Time: 10 minutes.  Makes 2 cups.

1/3 cup rock salt (*sanchal*)
3 cups white vinegar
½ cup carrots cubes
½ cup zucchini cubes
½ cup coloured capsicum cubes
½ cup cucumber cubes
½ cup beetroot slices
2 cloves garlic, crushed
2 green chillies, slit

1. Make the pickling solution, by boiling 2 cups of water with the rock salt.
2. Cool and add the vinegar. Mix well and keep aside.
3. Put all the vegetables, garlic and green chillies into a sterilized jar, fill the jar with

the pickling solution and seal with glass or plastic lids.
4. Store in a cool place for 1 week before using. Once opened, store in the refrigerator.
   Unopened pickled vegetables can be kept in a cool, dark place.
   Serve at room temperature.

*Main Course*

# Mixed Vegetable Stew

Picture on facing page.

*A stew with a difference. Vegetables simmered with baharat powder which results in a wholesome meal when served along with saffron rice. You can use ½ bread slice, crumbled instead of pita bread.*

Preparation Time: 10 minutes.   Cooking Time: 25 minutes.   Serves 4.

2 tbsp oil
½ cup finely chopped onions
1 tsp finely chopped garlic
½ tsp baharat, page 101
½ cup potato cubes
½ cup finely chopped tomatoes
¼ cup French beans, cut into 1" pieces
¼ cup zucchini slices
1 tbsp tomato purée
½ tsp cumin seeds (*jeera*) powder

**SAFFRON RICE : Recipe on page 77 ● MIXED VEGETABLE STEW : Recipe above.** ↪

½ tsp coriander (*dhania*) powder
Salt to taste
½ cup pita bread, page 99, pieces

**For serving**
Saffron rice, page 77

1. Heat the oil in a pan, add the onions and garlic and sauté till the onions turn translucent.
2. Add the baharat and potatoes and sauté for 5 minutes.
3. Add the tomatoes, French beans, zucchini and tomato purée and sauté for 2 more minutes.
4. Add the cumin seeds powder, coriander powder, salt and 3 cups of water. Mix well and bring to boil.
5. Lower the flame, add the bread pieces and simmer for 5 minutes. Serve hot with saffron rice.

# Stuffed Onion Cups

*A distinctive kind of baked dish where onion shells are baked with a rich mixture of rice, paneer and cashewnuts.*

Preparation Time: 10 minutes.  Cooking Time: 25 minutes.  Makes 5-6 onion cups.
Baking Temperature: 200°C (400°F).  Baking Time: 12-15 minutes.

2 large onions
1 tbsp oil
½ cup chopped tomatoes
½ cup cooked rice
½ cup grated *paneer* (cottage cheese)
2 tbsp chopped cashewnuts (*kaju*)
2 tbsp tomato purée
2 tbsp chopped parsley
½ tsp baharat, page 101
Salt to taste
½ tsp sugar

2 tbsp grated cheese for the topping
Oil for greasing

1. Peel the onions, trim off the roots and top and cut into halves.
2. Separate the outer layer of the onion halves from the smaller central layers and discard the latter. Keep the outer halves aside.
3. Heat the oil in a pan add the tomatoes and sauté for 2 minutes.
4. Add all the remaining ingredients and sauté for 5 to 6 more minutes.
5. Stuff the onion halves with the above mixture and top with the cheese.
6. Arrange the onion cups on a greased baking dish and bake in a pre-heated hot oven at 200°C (400°F) for 8 to 10 minutes or till the cheese melts.
   Serve hot.

# Stuffed Tomato

*A rare combination of tomatoes with dry fruits. The rich dry fruit stuffing is assembled in tomato shells and baked till the shells are soft and moist to bite into. If using large tomatoes, cut them lengthwise and scoop the halves to stuff the mixture.*

Preparation Time: 10 minutes.  Cooking Time: 10 minutes.  Serves 4.
Baking Temperature: 200°C (400°F).  Baking Time: 10-12 minutes.

4 medium sized firm tomatoes
1 tbsp oil
½ cup finely chopped onions
1 tbsp finely chopped garlic
½ cup cooked rice
½ cup grated *paneer* (cottage cheese)
¼ cup chopped nuts (cashewnuts and almonds)
3 tbsp raisins (*kismis*)
2 tbsp tomato purée
2 tbsp chopped parsley
½ tsp baharat, page 101

½ tsp turmeric powder (*haldi*)
Salt to taste
½ tsp sugar
2 tbsp grated cheese for the topping
Oil for greasing

1. Cut the tops off the tomatoes and scoop out the pulp. Keep both the tomatoes and the pulp aside.
2. Heat the oil in a pan, add the onions and garlic and sauté till the onions turn translucent.
3. Add all the remaining ingredients including the tomato pulp and sauté for 5-6 minutes.
4. Fill the scooped tomatoes with the above mixture and top with the cheese.
5. Grease the outer surface of the stuffed tomatoes with the oil.
6. Arrange the stuffed tomatoes on a greased baking dish and bake in a pre-heated oven at 200°C (400°F) for 5-7 minutes or till the cheese melts.
   Serve hot.

# Borëk

*Yes, these are the all-time-favourite baked potatoes which are spiced with the traditional baharat powder to let the recipe find place in this book. Spinach is not added in the original baked potatoes, but here it imparts a flavour liked by the Lebanese thus it is included.*

Preparation Time: 25 minutes.  Cooking Time: 30 minutes.  Serves 4.
Baking Temperature: 230°C (460°F).  Baking Time: 15 to 20 minutes.

4 medium size potatoes, boiled and peeled
2 tbsp butter
¼ cup chopped onions
1 tbsp chopped garlic
½ cup shredded spinach (*palak*)
½ cup fresh cream
¼ cup grated cheese
Salt to taste
2 tsp baharat, page 101

1. Cut the potatoes into thick roundels and keep aside.

2. Heat the butter in a pan, add the onions and garlic and sauté till the onions turn golden brown.
3. Add the spinach and sauté for 2 minutes.
4. Add 2 tbsp of cream, cheese and salt, mix well and cook on a low flame for 3-4 minutes till the sauce thickens. Keep aside.
5. Grease a 150 mm. (6") x 100 mm. (4") diameter dish and spread half the potato roundels on it.
6. Pour ¼ cup of cream and sprinkle 1 tsp of baharat and salt over it.
7. Spread the spinach mixture over it and then the remaining potato roundels over it.
8. Top with the remaining cream, cheese and baharat.
9. Bake in a pre-heated oven at 230°C (460°F) for 10 to 15 minutes.
   Serve hot.

# Stuffed Zucchini

**Picture on page 65.**

*A continental recipe which has been customized with ingredients like pine nuts, parsley and mint leaves to transform into a Lebanese delicacy. Instead of zucchini you can try using bottle gourd or cucumber.*

Preparation Time: 25 minutes.  Cooking Time: 60 minutes.  Serves 4.
Baking Temperature: 200°C (400°F).  Baking Time: 15-17 minutes.
Soaking time : 15 minutes.

**For the white sauce**
2 tsp butter
1 tsp plain flour (*maida*)
¾ cup milk
Salt and freshly ground pepper to taste

**Other ingredients**
4 nos. zucchini
½ cup long grained rice (*basmati*)
2 tbsp oil
1 tbsp pine nuts (chilgoza)

1 tsp chopped garlic
½ cup finely chopped onions
Salt to taste
1 cup grated *paneer* (cottage cheese)
1 tsp chopped mint leaves (*phudina*)
½ tsp baharat, page 101
1 tbsp chopped parsley
½ tsp freshly ground pepper
½ cup grated cheese for the topping
Oil for greasing

**For the white sauce**
1. Heat the butter in a pan, add the plain flour and cook on a slow flame while stirring throughout, until froth appears.
2. Add the milk gradually and stir continuously until the sauce thickens.
3. Add the salt and pepper and mix well. Keep aside.

**STUFFED ZUCCHINI : Recipe on page 63.** →

**How to proceed**

1. Cut the zucchini into 2 lengthwise. Scoop out the seeds and discard them.
2. Blanch the zucchini halves in salted hot water. Keep aside.
3. Clean, wash and soak the rice for 15 minutes. Drain and keep aside.
4. Put 1 cup of water to boil.
5. Heat the oil in a pan, add the pine nuts, garlic and onions and sauté till the onions turn translucent.
6. Add the rice and sauté for 2 minutes.
7. Add the hot water and salt and cook on a medium flame till the rice is almost done.
8. Add all the remaining ingredients except the zucchini, mix gently and cook till the rice is tender.
9. Fill the zucchini halves with the above mixture and arrange them on a greased baking tray.
10. Spoon out the white sauce over it and top with the cheese.
11. Bake in a pre-heated oven for 10-12 minutes or till the cheese melts.
    Serve hot.

# Lebanese Sizzler

*Succulent falafel patties combined with bean and spinach rice topped with hot sauce and vegetables are assembled to give you a sizzling extravagance.*

Preparation Time: 20 minutes.   Cooking Time: 45 minutes.   Makes 2 sizzlers.

1 recipe bean and spinach rice, page 81
1 recipe falafel, page 13
Oil for deep-frying
2 tbsp oil mixed with ½ cup water

**For the vegetables in hot sauce**
4 large tomatoes, blanched and peeled
2 tsp chilli powder
3 cloves garlic
1 tbsp oil
¼ cup finely chopped spring onion whites
½ tsp roasted cumin seeds (*jeera*) powder
2 tbsp tomato ketchup
Salt to taste

2 cups mixed boiled vegetables (zucchini, carrots, mushrooms, brinjal etc.), cut into cubes
½ cup finely chopped spring onion greens

### For the vegetables in hot sauce
1. Blend the tomatoes, chilli powder and garlic in a mixer to a smooth pureé. Keep aside.
2. Heat the oil in a pan, add the spring onion whites and sauté till they turn translucent.
3. Add the prepared purée, cumin seeds powder, tomato ketchup and salt and cook till the mixture leaves oil.
4. Add the mixed vegetables and simmer for 2 to 3 minutes.
5. Add the spring onion greens and mix well. Keep aside.

### How to proceed
1. Heat 2 sizzler plates over an open flame till they are red hot. Place them on their respective wooden trays.
2. Arrange half of the bean and spinach rice on the hot sizzler plate.
3. Pour half the vegetable hot sauce over it.
4. Place half the falafels on one side of the sizzler plate.
5. Repeat with the remaining ingredients to make one more sizzler.
6. Pour the oil-water mixture over the cast iron plates for a sizzling effect. Serve immediately.

 Rice

# *Mashkool Rice*

*Long grained rice tossed with deep-fried potatoes, onions and tomatoes and generously seasoned with baharat powder.*

Preparation Time: 15 minutes.   Cooking Time: 25 minutes.   Serves 4.
Soaking Time: 15 minutes.

Oil for deep-frying
1 cup sliced potatoes
1 cup sliced onions
¾ cup sliced tomatoes
1¼ cups long grained rice (*basmati*)
Salt to taste
4 tbsp ghee (*samneh*)
½ tsp baharat, page 101
½ tsp cumin seeds (*jeera*) powder
3 tbsp milk
2 tbsp rose water

1. Heat the oil in a *kadhai* and deep-fry the potatoes on a medium flame till they are cooked and golden brown. Drain on absorbent paper and keep aside.
2. In the same oil, deep-fry the onions till golden brown. Drain on absorbent paper and keep aside.
3. Put 3 tbsp of the above hot oil in a pan, add the tomatoes and cook on both sides on a high flame for 2 minutes. Drain on absorbent paper and keep aside.
4. Clean, wash and soak the rice for 15 minutes.
5. Boil a vesselful of water. Add the rice and salt and cook till rice is done (approx.10 minutes). Drain and keep aside.
6. Heat the ghee in a *kadhai,* add the rice, half the fried onions, potatoes, tomatoes, baharat, cumin seeds powder, milk, rose water and salt and mix gently.
   Serve hot garnished with the remaining fried onions.

# Mumawash Rice

*A Lebanese khichdi flavoured with whole garam masalas. Rose water and milk add richness to the preparation.*

Preparation Time: 15 minutes.   Cooking Time: 45 minutes.   Serves 4.
Soaking Time: 10 minutes.

Oil for deep-frying
¼ cup sliced onions
1¼ cups long grained rice (*basmati*)
½ cup masoor dal (*split red lentils*)
2 tbsp ghee (*samneh*)
½ cup chopped onions
½ tsp baharat, page 101
50 mm. (2″) cinnamon sticks (*dalchini*)
2 cloves (*laung / lavang*)
4 whole peppercorns
4 cardamoms (*elaichi*)
3 tbsp milk

2 tbsp rose water
Salt to taste

1. Heat the oil in a *kadhai* and deep-fry the onion slices on a medium flame till they are golden brown. Drain on absorbent paper and keep aside for the garnish.
2. Clean, wash and soak the rice and *masoor dal* separately for 10 minutes. Drain and keep aside.
3. Put 4 cups of water to boil.
4. Heat the ghee in a broad pan, add the onions and garlic and sauté till the onions are translucent.
5. Add the rice and *masoor dal* and sauté for 5 minutes.
6. Add the hot water and simmer for 5 minutes.
7. Add all the remaining ingredients, except the fried onions, cover with a lid and cook till the rice and *dal* are done.
8. Remove the cinnamon and cloves and discard them.
9. Separate each grain of rice lightly with a fork.
   Serve hot garnished with fried onions.

# Date and Rice Pilaf

Picture on facing page.

*Dates are an all time favourite with Middle Eastern countries. Here cooked with rice it creates an appetizing recipe.*

Preparation Time: 10 minutes.   Cooking Time: 20 minutes.   Serves 4.
Soaking Time: 15 minutes.

Oil for deep-frying
¼ cup sliced onions
1¼ cups long grained rice (*basmati*)
3 tbsp ghee (*samneh*)
Salt to taste
¼ cup almonds (*badam*)
¼ cup chopped seedless dates
¼ cup raisins (*kismis*)
1 tbsp rose water
2 tbsp milk

**DATE AND RICE PILAF : Recipe above.** ↪

½ tsp cardamom (*elaichi*) powder
1 tbsp chopped coriander (*dhania*) for the garnish

1. Heat the oil in a *kadhai* and deep-fry the onion slices on a medium flame till they are golden brown. Drain on absorbent paper and keep aside for the garnish.
2. Clean, wash and soak the rice for 15 minutes.
3. Boil a vesselful of water with the salt. Drain the rice, add it to the water and cook till the rice is done (approx.10 minutes). Drain again and keep aside.
4. Heat the ghee in a pan add the almonds and fry till they turn golden brown.
5. Add the dates, raisins, cooked rice, rosewater, milk and cardamom powder. Mix gently and cook for 5 minutes.
   Serve hot garnished with coriander and fried onions.

# Saffron Rice

Picture on page 55.

*Very similar to Indian style saffron rice only addition is rose water and nuts.*

Preparation Time: 15 minutes.   Cooking Time: 45 minutes.   Serves 4.
Soaking Time: 15 minutes.

Oil for deep-frying
¼ cup sliced onions
1¼ cups long grained rice (*basmati*)
Salt to taste
2 tbsp ghee (*samneh*)
¼ cup chopped onions
¼ cup sliced almonds (*badam*)
¼ cup raisins (*kismis*)
½ tsp saffron (*kesar*) soaked in ½ cup of rose water
3 tbsp milk

**For serving**
Mixed vegetable stew, page 54

1. Heat the oil in a *kadhai* and deep-fry the onion slices on a medium flame till they are golden brown. Drain on absorbent paper and keep aside.
2. Clean, wash and soak the rice for 15 minutes.
3. Boil a vesselful of water. Add the rice and salt and cook till rice is done (approx.10 minutes). Drain and keep aside.
4. Heat the ghee in a pan, add the onions, almonds and raisins and sauté till the onions turn golden brown.
5. Lower the flame and add the cooked rice, saffron-rose water mixture, milk, fried onions and salt.
6. Mix gently, cover the pan with a lid and cook for 5 minutes.
   Serve hot with mixed vegetable stew.

# Vermicelli Rice

*Vermicelli is used extensively in Lebanese cooking to make both sweet and savoury dishes. The same recipe can be converted into a sweet by cooking the rice with milk and little sugar.*

Preparation Time: 15 minutes.   Cooking Time: 45 minutes.   Serves 4.
Soaking Time: 15 minutes.

1¼ cups long grained rice (*basmati*)
½ cup fine vermicelli, broken into 2" pieces
¼ cup ghee (*samneh*)
Salt to taste

**For serving**
Mixed Vegetable Stew, page 54

1. Clean the rice and soak in water for 15 minutes. Drain and keep aside.
2. Put 3 cups of water to boil.
3. Heat the ghee in a broad pan, add the vermicelli and sauté till it becomes golden brown.

4. Add the rice and sauté for 2 to 3 minutes.
5. Add the water and salt and bring to boil.
6. Lower the flame, cover the pan with a lid and simmer till the rice is cooked (approx. 20 to 25 minutes).
   Serve hot with mixed vegetable stew.

# Bean and Spinach Rice

*Spinach pooled with kidney beans and rice delicately flavoured with cumin seeds powder. One serving will give you a nourishing supply of protein, folic acid and iron.*

Preparation Time: 15 minutes.   Cooking Time: 45 minutes.   Serves 4.
Soaking Time: 15 minutes.

1¼ cups long grained rice (*basmati*)
Salt to taste
1 tbsp oil
2 cloves garlic, grated
1 green chilli, finely chopped
1 cup finely chopped spinach (*palak*)
½ cup boiled and cooked *rajma* (kidney beans)
½ tsp roasted cumin seeds (*jeera*) powder

1. Clean, wash and soak the rice for 15 minutes.
2. Boil a vesselful of water. Add the rice and salt and cook till rice is done (approx.10 minutes). Drain and keep aside.

3. Heat the oil in a pan, add the garlic and green chillies and sauté for a few seconds.
4. Add the spinach, *rajma* and salt and sauté for 3 to 4 minutes.
5. Add the rice and cumin seeds powder and toss well.
   Serve hot.

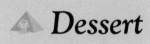 *Dessert*

# *Baklava*

**Picture on facing page.**

*World famous dessert from Middle Eastern countries. Each country in this region has its own recipe for baklava. There are many combinations and variations for this sinfully calorie laden dessert. Samosa pattis have been used instead of the filo pastry as the latter is not easily available in India.*

Preparation Time: 25 minutes.   Cooking Time: 20 minutes.   Makes 4.

4 ready-made frozen *samosa pattis*
Oil for deep-frying
Honey for drizzling

**For the filling**
¼ cup chopped walnuts (*akhrot*)
¼ cup soaked and chopped figs (*anjeer*)
¼ cup soaked and chopped apricots (*kuumani / jardalu*)
¼ cup chopped dates (*khajur*)
¼ tsp cinnamon (*dalchini*) powder
2 tbsp honey

**BAKLAVA: Recipe above.** ↝

2 tbsp brown sugar
1 tsp lemon juice

1. Cut each *samosa patti* into 3 to get 75 mm. x 62 mm. (3" x 2½") rectangles. You will get 12 pieces in all.
2. Heat the oil in a *kadhai* and deep-fry the *samosa pattis* till golden brown. Drain on absorbent paper and keep aside.
3. Mix all the ingredients for the filling together and divide into 8 equal portions. Keep aside.
4. Place one *samosa patti* piece on a flat surface and place one portion of the filling on it taking care to leave the sides clean.
5. Place another piece of *samosa patti* on top.
6. Put another portion of the filling on it again taking care to leave the sides clean.
7. Top with the third piece of the *samosa patti*.
8. Repeat with the remaining *samosa pattis* and filling to make 3 more baklavas. Drizzle honey on top and serve immediately.

# Chocolate and Date Mousse

*A delicious, elegant no-fuss dessert.*

Preparation Time: 10 minutes.   Cooking Time: 5 minutes.   Serves 4.

10 dates
1 tsp *samneh* (ghee)
1 cup (125 grams) dark chocolate, chopped
1 cup (200 grams) fresh cream
¼ cup chopped black dates
2 tbsp chopped walnuts (*akhrot*)

1. Combine the dates and ghee in a small pan and sauté for 1-2 minutes.
2. Cool, add ¼ cup of milk and blend inn a mixer to a coarse paste. Keep aside.
3. Combine the chocolate and 2 tbsp of milk in a small bowl and melt over a double boiler till it is a smooth mixture. Do not stir vigourously. Cool slightly.
4. Add the dates mixture and mix gently.
5. Whip the cream till soft peaks form and fold it into the date- chocolate mixture.

6. Add the walnuts and chopped dates and mix again.
7. Pour this mixture into 4 long stemmed glasses.
8. Refrigerate for 4 to 6 hours or till the mousse has set.
   Serve chilled.

# Nutty Caramel Cigars

*Crisp rolls with a date and nut stuffing, deep-fried and served with hot caramel sauce drizzled over it.*

Preparation Time: 15 minutes.   Cooking Time: 10 minutes.   Makes 18 cigars.

6 ready-made frozen *samosa pattis*
1 tbsp plain flour (*maida*) mixed with 1 tbsp water
Oil for deep-frying

**For the caramel sauce**
1 cup sugar
2 tbsp oil

**For the filling**
1 tbsp ghee (*samneh*)
½ cup chopped seedless black dates (*khajur*)
¼ cup finely chopped mixed nuts (cashewnuts, pistachios, almonds and walnuts)

**For the caramel sauce**
1. Combine the sugar, oil and ½ cup of water in a pan and cook over a high flame till the mixture starts bubbling.
2. Lower the flame and allow the mixture to caramelize without stirring. If required shake the pan gently to prevent the sugar from burning around the edges of the pan.
3. When the syrup is light brown in colour, remove from the flame. Keep warm.

**For the filling**
1. Heat the ghee in a pan, add the dates and sauté for 2 minutes.
2. Cool and blend in a mixer to a smooth paste.
3. Add the mixed nuts and mix well.
4. Divide the mixture into 18 equal portions and keep aside.

**How to proceed**
1. Cut each *samosa patti* into 3 to get 75 mm. x 62 mm. (3" x 2½") rectangular pieces. You will get 18 pieces in all.
2. Place one *samosa patti* piece on a flat surface and place one portion of the filling at one corner. Roll it up tightly starting from the end where the filling is placed to make a cigar.

3. Seal the edge of the *samosa patti* piece using a little of the plain flour paste.
4. Repeat with the remaining *pattis* and filling to make 17 more cigars.
5. Heat the oil in a *kadhai* and deep-fry the cigars till golden brown. Drain on absorbent paper.

Serve hot with caramel sauce.

# Lebanese Fresh Fruit Salad

*Cubes of fresh garden fruits tossed with honey and garnished with fresh mint leaves. For best results serve chilled.*

Preparation Time: 15 minutes.   Cooking Time: Nil.   Serves 4.

2 tbsp lemon juice
1 cup muskmelon (*kharbooja*) cubes
½ cup pineapple cubes
½ cup peeled oranges, cut into pieces
½ cup apple cubes
½ cup strawberries, halved
¼ black grapes, halved
¼ cup green grapes, halved
1 tbsp honey for drizzling
3-4 mint leaves (*phudina*) leaves for the garnish

1. Combine all the ingredients in a mixing bowl and toss well.
2. Drizzle the honey on top.
3. Garnish with mint leaves and refrigerate till use. Serve chilled.

*Beverages*

# Apple Tea

*Lebanese people are great lovers of tea, specially the fruit flavoured teas. In Lebanon, apple flavoured tea leaves are readily available but try the following recipe to make a home-made version.*

Preparation Time: 5 minutes. Cooking Time: 10 minutes. Serves 4.

2 tsp green tea leaves
1 apple, peeled and cut into slices
4 tsp sugar

½ tsp lemon juice
½ tsp cinnamon (*dalchini*) powder

1. Put the tea leaves in a kettle and keep aside.
2. Combine all the remaining ingredients in a pan with 5 cups of water and bring to boil.
3. Lower the flame and simmer for 3-4 minutes.
4. Strain into the kettle and keep aside for a couple of minutes so that the flavours blend well.
   Serve hot.

**Variation** : *Pomegranate Tea*

Use 1 cup of pomegranate instead of apples and avoid the use of cinnamon powder.

# Ginger and Milk Drink

*A quick drink made using handy ingredients ideal to fight cold.*

Preparation Time: 5 minutes.   Cooking Time: 20 minutes.   Serves 4.

2 tbsp grated ginger
4 cups milk
4 tsp sugar
3-4 mint (*phudina*) leaves for the garnish

1. Combine the ginger and 3 cups of water in a pan and bring to boil.
2. Lower the flame and simmer for 10-15 minutes until a hot yellow liquid is formed.
   Strain and keep aside.
3. Boil the milk in a pan.
4. Remove from the flame, add the strained liquid and sugar and mix well.
   Serve hot garnished with mint leaves.

# Ayraan

*A Lebanese equivalent of Chaas, the only difference being this has a pungent flavour of garlic.*

Preparation Time: 1-2 minutes.   Cooking Time: Nil.   Makes 4 glasses.

2 cups fresh curds (*dahi*), made from full fat milk
1 cup full fat milk
1 tsp finely chopped garlic
Salt to taste
4-5 ice-cubes to serve

1. Combine all the ingredients except the ice-cubes and blend in a mixer for 3-4 minutes.
2. Pour into 4 individual glasses and serve immediately.

# *Lemon Cooler*

*A refreshing lemon drink enhanced with the addition of rose water and mint leaves.*

Preparation Time: 1-2 minutes.   Cooking Time: Nil.   Makes 4 glasses.

6 tbsp sugar
6 tbsp lemon juice
A few drops of rose water
4-6 ice-cubes
A few mint leaves (*phudina*) for the garnish

1. Combine the sugar and ½ cup of water in a pan and simmer till the sugar is dissolved.
2. Remove from the flame and keep aside to cool.
3. Add the lemon juice, rose water, ice-cubes and 3 cups of water and blend in a mixer till frothy.
4. Pour into 4 individual glasses and serve chilled garnished with mint leaves.

*Basic Recipes*

# *Pita Bread*

**Picture on cover.**

*Yes, this famous bread is from Lebanon. Unique bread which, forms a pocket while baking is used to accompany any dish in the Lebanese cuisine. Traditionally baked in an oven, but I have suggested a recipe using the tava. Now-a-days many bakeries sell pita bread so if you choose to get it from the market always ask for soft and freshly baked pita. It can be stored for a few days wrapped in a plastic bag and kept in the freezer.*

Preparation Time: 15 minutes.   Cooking Time: 10 minutes.   Makes 12 breads.

¾ cup whole wheat flour (*gehun ka atta*)
¾ tsp crumbled fresh yeast
½ tsp sugar
1 tbsp oil
½ tsp salt

1. Combine all the ingredients, except the oil and salt in a bowl and knead into a soft dough using enough water.
2. Add the oil and salt and knead again till it is smooth and elastic.

3. Cover the dough with a wet muslin cloth and allow it to prove till it doubles in volume (approx. 15 to 20 minutes).
4. Press the dough lightly to remove the air.
5. Divide the dough into 6 equal parts and roll out each portion into a oblong of 150 mm. (6") length and 6 mm. (¼") thickness.
6. Cook the pita breads on a hot *tava* (griddle) over medium flame on each side for a minute or until the bread puffs up and a cavity is created in the bread.
7. Cut each pita bread into 2 halves and use as required.

# Baharat

*A Lebanese spice mix prepared and kept handy like our garam masalas.*

Preparation Time: 1-2 minutes.   Cooking Time: Nil.   Makes approx. 1 cup.

¼ cup black pepper
¼ cup red chilli flakes *(paprika)*
1 tbsp coriander *(dhania)* seeds
1 tbsp cinnamon *(dalchini)*
1 tbsp cumin seeds *(jeera)*
1 tbsp cloves *(laung / lavang)*
1 tbsp nutmeg *(jaiphal)*
1 tbsp dry ginger *(soonth)* powder
1 tbsp green cardamom *(elaichi)*

1. Dry roast all the ingredients on a *tava* (griddle) till they release an aroma. Keep aside to cool.
2. Blend in a mixer to a fine powder and store in an air-tight container.
   Use as required.

# Vegetable Stock

*A basic recipe that adds flavour to lots of soups and gravies.*

Preparation Time: 10 minutes.   Cooking Time: 10 minutes.   Makes 3 cups.

½ cup roughly chopped cabbage
½ cup roughly chopped carrots
2 tbsp chopped celery
2 tbsp chopped spring onions
3 to 4 cauliflower florets
3-4 cloves (*laung / lavang*)
25 mm (1") stick cinnamon (*dalchini*)
1 bayleaf (*tejpatta*)
Salt to taste

1. Boil all the ingredients in 4 cups of water on a medium flame for 15 to 20 minutes, till it reduces to about 3 cups.
2. Allow the vegetables to settle at the bottom of the vessel and drain out the stock.
3. Discard the vegetables and use the stock as required.

*A magazine by* **TARLA DALAL**

*Book your copy now...*

Price : Rs. 50/-

Available at your nearest bookstore, newspaper stands and tarladalal.com

# SUBSCRIBE NOW & Get Free
# Bonus Membership at tarladalal.com

Pick any one of the subscription offers and send us a cheque or a Demand Draft in favour of "Sanjay & Co." along with your detailed address including pin code, telephone no. and e-mail address.

Addressed to :

Sanjay & Co. 353, A-1, Shah & Nahar Industrial Estate, Dhanraj Mill Compound, Lower Parel (W), Mumbai 400013. INDIA

5 years (30 issues) + 1 Year Free Membership = Rs. 1450/-*

3 Years (18 issues) + 9 Months Free Membership = Rs. 1080/-*

1 Year (6 issues) + 2 Months Free Membership = Rs. 340/-*

**\*Offer valid for shipments only within India and is inclusive of shipping & handling charges.**

For overseas shipments log on to tarladalal.com

For more information, call us on our helpline no. (022) 2496 8068 on all weekdays between 9.30 a.m. and 4.30 p.m. or write to us at subscription@tarladalal.com

# Mini Series by *Tarla Dalal*

7 Dinner Menus

Forever Young Diet

Nutritious Recipes
for Pregnancy

Healthy Subzis

High Blood Pressure
Cookbook

Low Calorie Sweets

Good Food for Diabetes

Healthy Snacks for Kids

Iron Rich Recipes

Low Cholesterol Recipes

Healthy Juices

Healthy Breakfast

Healthy Snacks

Healthy Soups & Salads

Calcium Rich Recipes

Home Remedies

Fast Foods made Healthy